A is for Aloha

A Hawai'i Alphabet

Written by U'ilani Goldsberry and Illustrated by Tammy Yee

Sleeping Bear Press

310 North Main Street, Suite 300
Chelsea, MI 48118
www.sleepingbearpress.com

THOMSON

GALE

© 2005 Thomson Gale, a part of the Thomson Corporation.

Thomson, Star Logo and Sleeping Bear Press are trademarks
and Gale is a registered trademark used herein under license.

Printed and bound in Canada.

10 9 8 7 6 5 4 3 2 1

Library of Congress Cataloging-in-Publication Data

Goldsberry, U'ilani.
A is for aloha : a Hawai'i alphabet / written by U'ilani Goldsberry ;
illustrated by Tammy Yee.
p. cm.
ISBN 1-58536-146-1
1. Hawaii—Juvenile literature. 2. English language—Alphabet—
Juvenile literature. I. Yee, Tammy, ill. II. Title.
DU623.25.G65 2005
996.9—dc22   2005005887

*For my wonderful children, Micah, Haunani, and Pancho, and to little Kirra,
the most beautiful granddaughter in the world. Root yourselves in the core
of these islands. They are your center. Your balance. Your home.*

*And for my husband Steven, whose love, understanding, and support
have sustained me these past 30 years.*

U'ILANI

✿

To Ric, Cosmo, and Bobby, the three boys in my life.

TAMMY

With a single word, Hawaiians can express feelings of love, compassion, mercy, kindness, charity, regards, affection, hello, and good-bye. The word *ku'u* means "my." Add *aloha*, and you have *ku'u aloha*, or "my love." The origin of the word *aloha* is lost in the shadows of ancient Hawai'i. But if we break the word down, *alo* means "to be in the presence of," and *ha* is "the breath of life:" to be in the presence of life. *Aloha* is vital to the Hawaiian way of life. This one word communicates all of the traditions of care and generosity that make Hawai'i such a special place.

A is also for the Aloha Tower. In the early 1900s, travel to and from the islands was done entirely by steamship. The people of Honolulu built the tower on the harborside of the piers to greet passengers or send them home with a fond farewell. The building was originally used as a maritime communications and harbor control center. Today the observation deck is open to the public.

A is for Aloha

Aloha is our letter A.
It means so many things:
hello, good-bye, and love to you.
Fair wishes this word brings.

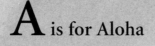

BISHOP MUSEUM

In 1957 the nēnē goose became our state bird. This distant cousin of the Canadian goose is brown, with black and white feathers lined up in diagonal rows. Scientists believe that the nēnē were blown off course during one of their migratory journeys from Canada to Mexico, and landed on the islands of Hawai'i. Today, the nēnē lives on the slopes of the great volcanoes, and is on the list of endangered species.

B is also for the Bishop Museum, established in 1889 by Charles Reed Bishop to honor his late wife, Princess Bernice Pauahi, the last descendant of the royal Kamehameha family. Her final wish was to help Hawai'i's children develop a greater pride in their heritage. Located near downtown Honolulu, the museum is the largest in the state, and has over 25 million items that tell the natural and cultural history of the islands, including ancient wooden surfboards, canoes, finely carved tikis, and royal feather capes. The exhibits tell the story of the extinct and endangered plants and animals.

B is for state Bird

The nēnē is a Hawaiian goose,
with feathers beige and brown.
It lives atop the great volcanoes
and never goes to town.

Bb

C is for Capital

Hawai'i's capital, Honolulu,
    is like a jewel so bright.
It shines against the lush green mountains,
and sparkles in the night.

Honolulu is Hawai'i's capital city, on the Island of O'ahu. The word *Honolulu* means "protected bay." The city and county of Honolulu is the biggest—by area—in the world. Its land stretches out nearly 1,500 miles long, because it includes all of the islands north of Ni'ihau up to Kure Atoll. The city of Honolulu lies on O'ahu's south shore. It was once called "the white city" because of all its coral buildings. With a population of 879,156, Honolulu is the 11th largest city in the United States.

C is also for our state capitol building in downtown Honolulu, which was designed to resemble a volcano. Forty large pillars support the roof and represent coconut palms, and the eight smaller pillars that hold up the top floor symbolize Hawai'i's eight major islands: Hawai'i, Kaho'olawe, Kaua'i, Lāna'i, Maui, Moloka'i, Ni'ihau, and O'ahu. The main courtyard opens to the sky with a domed top in the shape of a volcanic cinder cone, and a reflecting pool that represents the Pacific Ocean surrounds the entire building.

The ancient Hawaiians didn't have a written language. So they chanted their stories, and to add drama they danced. The hula portrayed tales of heroism and harvest, god-worship, and fertility. They were passionate dances done by torchlight. When Christian missionaries came to Hawai'i, they did not understand the hula, and they didn't like Hawaiians worshipping the ancient gods. The missionaries made the hula illegal for anyone to practice or dance. Today, when you come to the islands, you'll see the ancient or *kahiko* hula (performed to the sound of drums and chanting), and the modern or *'auana* hula (with smoother movements, and guitars and singing).

D is also for drums. The ancient Hawaiians used drums of all sizes. Small ones sounded like heavy rain on a grass-thatched roof, and large ones rumbled like booming thunder. Chanters used a *pahu* made from a partially hollowed-out tree trunk and topped with tightly stretched sharkskin to pound out a steady beat for their dancers. They also used a small *pūniu*, or coconut knee-drum, made from a coconut shell, and covered in fish skin.

D is for the Dance of hula

There are two styles of hula,
    one older than the other.
Kahiko is the ancient one—
    'Auana is the younger.

E e

In Hawai'i, unlike most places in the United States, electricity is generated using oil-fueled turbines. But Hawai'i has worked to develop three different types of alternative energy: wind, hydro-electricity, and geothermal. The trade winds blow constantly against the mountains. Scientists trying to harness this infinite energy source have built a number of "wind farms" on the islands of Hawai'i, Kaua'i, and Maui that supply electricity to sugar mills and communities. Small generators also capture energy flowing from mountain streams on these islands to create hydroelectricity. And geothermal energy is produced by harvesting the trapped gases from deep within the active volcanoes on the island of Hawai'i.

E is also for the ancient energy of the *kukui*, or candlenut tree, our state tree. The old Hawaiians used this tree for many things. They strung a few kukui nuts together, then placed them in a lava-rock bowl, and lit wicks to make lamps to illuminate their houses. They also squeezed oil from the nuts, and used it as medicine, or chopped up the nutmeat to flavor their cooking.

E is for other forms of Energy

The trade winds sheer the ridges
and spin the windmills round.
They turn the energy of the sky
into electricity for our towns.

The state flower of Hawai'i is the yellow hibiscus. It symbolizes the delicate balance in the islands, and radiates the color of sunshine. In 1923 the Territory of Hawai'i named the hibiscus, all colors and varieties, its official flower. But in 1988 the state legislature decided that since the yellow hibiscus—or the *pua aloalo*—is one of only five hibiscus species native to the islands, it should be the one flower that proudly represents our beautiful state.

F is also for our state's unofficial fish called *humuhumunukunukuapua'a*. It is pronounced hoo-moo-hoo-moo-noo-koo-noo-koo-ah-poo-ah-ah. This little fish lives in the shallow reefs along the coasts of all of the Hawaiian Islands, and grows to be about 10 inches long. The Hawaiian word, *humuhumu* means "trigger fish" (for the trigger-like fin on its back). *Nukunuku* means "snout," *a* means "of," and *pua'a* means "pig." So, can you guess what he looks like?

F is for state Flower

Our F is the yellow hibiscus,
        so delicate and so fair.
Its hues are like the sunshine,
    a state flower beyond compare.

Ff

Our state gem, black coral, comes from the deep water beyond the reefs. Coral is actually the name of a group of marine animals related to jellyfish and sea anemones. Individually called polyps, these tube-like little creatures live together in colonies. In the deep sea, live black coral isn't really black at all. It's sometimes yellow, green, or even orange. When the polyps are gone, their crusty houses turn a very, very dark brownish black.

G is also for the Hawaiian green sea turtle. Some people call them the "birds of the ocean" because of the way they fly through the water. Their flippers move in an up-and-down motion, like the wings of a bird. The Hawaiians named the sea turtles *honu*. Young *honu* live in the shallow reefs, eating the seaweed that grows there. Like the Hawaiian monk seal, the Hawaiian green sea turtle is on the endangered species list. You can see lots of green sea turtles when you snorkel in the reefs off of any of the islands. *Honu* aren't afraid of humans, and will come up close to watch you watch them.

Gg

G is for state Gem

The black coral of Hawai'i
grows in the deepest sea.
It's the color of young lava
and looks like a leafless tree.

H is for the *Hōkūleʻa*

Hawaiʻi's *Hōkūleʻa*
is a modern voyaging canoe.
It catches the wind in triangular sails
like the ancient ones used to do.

The Hawaiian voyaging canoe called the *Hōkūleʻa* was launched on March 8, 1975. This modern replica of the vessels that brought Polynesians to Hawaiʻi has traveled throughout the Pacific. It is a living school, used to teach young native Hawaiians the art of open-ocean navigation. In ancient times, navigators used the stars, the tides, currents, and the flight-paths of birds to find their way across the vast landscape of the Pacific. Since its maiden voyage, the *Hōkūleʻa* has been joined by two sister ships: the *Hawaiʻiloa* (christened in 1993), and the *Iosepa* (launched November 3, 2001).

H is also for *hōkū*. The ancient Polynesians who sailed to Hawaiʻi used their knowledge of star movement to find their way across the Pacific. They called this type of astronomy *aʻo hōkū. Aʻo* means "teaching," and *hōkū* means "star." Today, using 13 giant telescopes on the summit of the Big Island's Mauna Keʻa, scientists study those same stars. Honolulu has its own zenith star. It rises directly above the city, and is named "Arcturus."

H h

I i

I is for the I'olani Palace

I'olani Palace is
the home of Hawai'i's kings:
It's the only palace in America
where the echo of the monarchy rings.

I'olani Palace, the only royal palace on American soil, is located in downtown Honolulu next-door to the state capitol building. King David Kalākaua and his wife Queen Kapi'olani built the palace in 1882, and named it *I'olani*, which means "royal hawk." It cost the kingdom $360,000. The king loved to travel, and he designed his palace to look like his favorite castles in Europe. There are high ramparts and beautiful staircases made of koa wood. The I'olani Palace had electricity and telephones before the White House in Washington, D.C.

I is also for film industry. The opening montage for the 1970s television series *Hawaii Five-0* shows Detective Steve McGarrett (played by Jack Lord) standing in a fictional office at I'olani Palace. The movie and television industry has been in love with the islands since the attack on Pearl Harbor in 1945. At least five TV shows or feature films are shot on location in the islands each year. Some well-known movies include *Jurassic Park* and the James Bond thriller *Die Another Day*.

Hawai'i's favorite princess, Victoria Ka'iulani Kalaninuiahilapalapa Kawekiui Lunalilo, lived with her parents on a beautiful estate in Waikīkī called 'Ainahau. She loved the sweet-scented Chinese jasmine blossoms that were planted on the grounds of her home so much that she named these flowers *pīkake*, the Hawaiian word for "peacock," her favorite bird. Today, small, pearl-like *pīkake* buds are sewn into leis, and no one gives or receives them without remembering Ka'iulani.

J is also for Hawai'i's "jovial" King David Kalākaua. His nickname was "The Merrie Monarch" because he loved music, dancing, parties, and the finest food and drinks. He was the first monarch to circumnavigate the globe during his 'round the world tour in 1881. And when he came home, he built the I'olani Palace. The Hawaiian culture enjoyed a revival during King Kalākaua's reign. He encouraged his people to speak their native language, dance the hula, and celebrate their culture.

J j

J is for Jasmine

Princess Ka'iulani,
favored child of Hawai'i,
named jasmine blossoms for her peacocks,
and called them sweet *pīkake*.

When King Kamehameha I (Kamehameha the Great) set out to conquer the islands of Hawai'i, Maui, Lāna'i, Moloka'i, and O'ahu in 1795, he mounted cannons on his large double-hulled canoe, and won all of the battles. After he united the islands under his reign, the Kingdom of Hawai'i enjoyed a period of peace. Kamehameha created the legal system and used taxes to promote trade with America and European countries. When he died in 1819, his high priests followed ancient tradition and hid his bones to protect his *mana* (power). Kamehameha's final resting place remains a mystery.

K is also for Kamehameha's flag. Before becoming a state, Hawai'i was an independent kingdom. During his reign, Kamehameha flew the British Union Jack (a gift from Captain George Vancouver) above his royal residence. America wanted Kamehameha to be more neutral so he ordered a new flag made. The Hawaiian flag (now our state flag) has eight stripes of white, red, and blue. They represent the eight main islands of the Hawaiian chain. The Union Jack is in the upper left corner, a symbol of the King's friendship with Britain.

K is for King Kamehameha

King Kamehameha
enjoyed both honor and fame.
He united all the islands
under one benevolent reign.

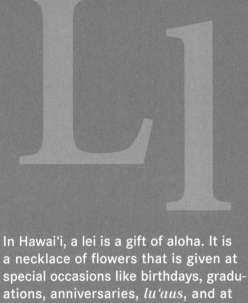

L is for Leis

Hawai'i's Leis begin with L,
sweet flowers sewn in garlands.
A ring of greeting and of love
that celebrate the islands.

In Hawai'i, a lei is a gift of aloha. It is a necklace of flowers that is given at special occasions like birthdays, graduations, anniversaries, *lu'aus*, and at farewell parties. The ancient Hawaiians even presented leis to their gods during solemn religious ceremonies, and farmers wore leis so that their crops would be blessed. Today, Hawai'i celebrates "Lei Day" on May 1st of every year. There are lei-making contests, and lots of parties. School children gather flowers and make leis to decorate the graves of fallen soldiers at the veterans' cemetery at Punchbowl Crater.

L is also for *lū'au*, a Hawaiian feast. Ancient Hawaiians called dinner *pā'ina* or *aha'aina*, not *lū'au*. *Lū'au* is the Hawaiian name for taro leaves that are used to wrap food before placing it in an *imu* (underground oven). In 1856, a newspaper writer described a Hawaiian feast and mistakenly called it a *lū'au*. The name stuck. Most *lū'aus* offer Hawaiian specialties like *kālua* pig, *lomi-lomi* salmon, poi, and *haupia* (a type of coconut pudding). But, since some visitors don't enjoy these traditional foods, modern menus also include American favorites like fried chicken, salad greens, teriyaki beef, and chocolate cake.

M m

Each year, from late November to mid-April, humpback whales migrate to Hawaiian waters to breed, give birth, and nurse their young. Adult humpbacks grow to more than 40 feet long and weigh more than 40 tons. They usually congregate in the waters off Maui and along the Big Island's Kona coast.

M is also for monk seal. The ancient Hawaiians called them *'īlio-holo-i-ka-uaua*, which means "the dog that runs in the rough (seas)." These endangered seals are called "monk" because they look bald and have a fold of skin behind their heads that looks like a monk's hood. Monk seals live on the tiny islands and atolls that lie to the northwest of the main Hawaiian Islands.

M is for sea Mammals

Dolphins, seals, and whales,
mammals of the sea,
ply the channel waters
between the islands of Hawai'i.

N is for Natural Resources

Natural resources are letter N,
the exports of Hawai'i.
Pineapple, coffee, and sugarcane
help fuel our state's economy.

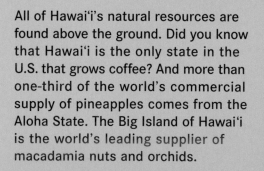

All of Hawai'i's natural resources are found above the ground. Did you know that Hawai'i is the only state in the U.S. that grows coffee? And more than one-third of the world's commercial supply of pineapples comes from the Aloha State. The Big Island of Hawai'i is the world's leading supplier of macadamia nuts and orchids.

N is also for newcomers. Ancient Hawaiians lived on these islands alone for thousands of years before Captain James Cook brought Westerners to Hawai'i. The Hawaiian name for newcomer is *malihini*. This word is used to describe a stranger, foreigner, tourist, guest, or someone who is visiting for the first time.

O is for Oʻahu

Most of Hawaiʻi's people
live on the island of Oʻahu.
They play in Waikīkī
and go to work in Honolulu.

The Hawaiian Islands

Niʻihau

Kauaʻi

Oʻahu

Molokaʻi

Maui

Lānaʻi

Kahoʻolawe

Hawaiʻi

Oʻahu
The Gathering Place

Honolulu

Waikiki

The island of Oʻahu is known as the "Gathering Place." It is the third-largest Hawaiian island, and the most densely populated. The state capital of Honolulu is located here, and so is the Honolulu International Airport. There are over 100 world-famous beaches on Oʻahu, along with one-third of the state's best surfing spots. The entire island is slightly larger than the city of Houston, Texas.

O is also for Hawaiʻi's Outer Islands, the nickname given to the other five large islands in the Hawaiian chain: Hawaiʻi, Maui, Lānaʻi, Molokaʻi, and Kauaʻi. All of the Hawaiian Islands are similar, but each has a nickname that distinguishes it from the others. The island of Hawaiʻi is called the "Big Island" for obvious reasons. It is twice the size of all the other Hawaiian Islands combined. Maui is called the "Valley Isle" because of the isthmus formed between the West Maui Mountains and Haleakalā Volcano. Lānaʻi is the "Secluded Island" because very few ships or planes stopped in for visits. Molokaʻi is the "Friendly Island," and Kauaʻi is the "Garden Island" because it receives over 500 inches of rain per year.

Polynesian voyagers, without the aid of a compass, navigated over 2,000 miles of open ocean nearly 1,000 years before Columbus. Relying on the migratory patterns of sea birds, varied coloration in the clouds, debris floating on the water, and the scent of exposed reefs, ancient mariners accurately directed their large double-hulled canoes to the Hawaiian Islands. Scientists believe that early migrations to Hawai'i originated from the Marquesas Islands, Raiatea in the Society Islands, and Samoa during the eleventh and twelfth centuries.

P is also for petroglyph, an ancient drawing etched into lava rock and stone. The Hawaiians called these images *ki'i pōhaku*, which means "stone carving." Petroglyphs are usually found in clusters like those on the Big Island in a place called Puakō, and near an old lighthouse on the island of Lāna'i. There are images of men, women, and children surfing, hunting, running, dancing, marching, traveling, and fishing. There are also little holes cut out of the rock where parents placed the umbilical cords of their newborns for good luck.

P is for the Polynesians

Polynesian explorers
braved the open sea.
Traveling through wind and blinding sun,
they discovered Hawai'i.

Q is for Queen

Hawai'i's last queen,
Lili'uokalani was her name,
lost her throne to businessmen
but her heart they could not claim.

Hawai'i's last reigning monarch, Queen Lili'uokalani, was born on September 2, 1838 in Honolulu. In 1891, her brother, King David Kalākaua died while on a trip to San Francisco, leaving the throne to Lili'uokalani. Her reign was very short. After four years, a group of American businessmen overthrew the Hawaiian government and placed the queen under arrest in I'olani Palace. With all her many accomplishments, Lili'uokalani is perhaps best remembered for writing the famous farewell song "Aloha 'Oe."

Another **Q** word is quilt. American missionaries from New England taught Hawaiian women to make blankets. They quickly developed the elaborate appliquéd flower, leaf, and vine designs that are now the hallmark of the Hawaiian quilt. But the most famous quilt in Hawai'i is one made by Queen Lili'uokalani. It is displayed in her "prison" room on the second floor of I'olani Palace. The "Queen's Quilt" documents her 10-month imprisonment.

The only tropical rain forests in the U.S. grow in Hawai'i. Many of our endangered species live in rain forest reserves on the islands of Kaua'i, O'ahu, Moloka'i, Maui, and on the Big Island. Here, silver raindrops hang suspended in the dense humid air, and rare birds like the endangered *'elepaio*, *'ōma'o*, and *'ākepa* flutter from branch to branch in the *'ōhi'a* and *kōlea lau nui* trees. Wild Hawaiian boars root for food amongst the tall *'ama'uma'u* ferns that grow along the forest floor. Remember that it takes lots of water to make a rain forest. It's a great place to get wet and muddy.

R is also for rainbows. In Hawai'i you can see half rainbows, full rainbows, double rainbows, triple rainbows, and even night rainbows illuminated by the full moon. Did you know that rainbows are always in front of you when your back is to the sun? Ancient Hawaiians believed that rainbows were bridges used by the gods when they visited the world of men.

R is for Rain Forest

Letter R is Rain Forest
that rises in the mists.
It is the home of native birds,
and legends, songs, and myths.

Rr

"Hawai'i Pono'ī," our state song, was written by King David Kalākaua and set to music by Professor Henry Berger, the Royal Bandmaster. The lyrics are written and sung in Hawaiian, and call all of Hawai'i's young men to be loyal to their chief, Kamehameha. It was first performed on November 16, 1874, in Honolulu's Kawaiaha'o Church, and became the official song of the Kingdom of Hawai'i, then the Territory of Hawai'i, and finally the State of Hawai'i.

S is also for statehood. At approximately 10:04 a.m. (Hawaiian Standard Time) on August 21, 1959, the United States House of Representatives voted 323 to 89 granting statehood to the Territory of Hawai'i, which became America's 50th state. Each year, on the third Friday in August, Hawai'i celebrates Statehood Day.

S s

S is for state Song

King Kalākaua wrote
"Hawai'i Pono'ī."
It calls upon Hawai'i's sons
to promise loyalty.

T t

Tsunami is the Japanese word that describes a wave so large that it fills an entire harbor, from the ocean floor to the top of the fishing boat masts. Giant landslides or massive underwater earthquakes create enormous waves that can travel hundreds of miles per hour. When these monsters get close to land, they hit the reef, suck out the water, and come crashing onto the shore. Hawai'i, located in the middle of the Pacific Ocean, is always on guard against these devastating waves.

T is also for the tide pools that form when the ocean covers the beach twice a day. In Hawai'i, tide pools are home to crabs, small fish, sea stars, sea cucumbers, and soft, waving beds of seaweed. All of the animals must be able to survive in both wet and dry conditions, because when low tide comes, the smaller pools turn warm, and begin to dry up.

T is for Tsunami

Tsunamis do not come
often to Hawai'i's shores.
But when they do, these giant waves
rise a hundred feet or more.

U is for Ukulele

Our U is Ukulele—
In Hawaiian it means "jumping flea."
When you play it, fingers jump so fast
on strings, from key to key.

In the summer of 1879, a ship carrying 400 Portuguese laborers arrived in Hawai'i. After sailing 15,000 miles in four months, a man named Joao Fernandes, from the island of Madeira, was so happy to finally be off the boat, he pulled out his friend's braguinha (a small guitar-like instrument), and started playing folk songs. The Hawaiians were so amazed at the way this strange little man's fingers jumped all over the fingerboard they called the little guitar 'ukulele, which means "jumping flea." Today the ukulele accompanies all of Hawai'i's music, and has gained international acclaim.

U is also for up-country, the pastures and open land on the slopes of the great volcanoes where the modern *paniolo* live. In 1838 King Kamehameha III invited California Spanish-Mexican *vaqueros* (cowboys) to teach Hawaiians how to manage the wild herds of long-horned steers brought to the islands by Captain George Vancouver. The Hawaiians called these cowboys *paniolo*, a word derived from "espanõl." The name was also given to the new Hawaiian cowboys.

U u

V v

Hawai'i sits atop the world's biggest mountain range, all made from volcanoes. The tallest peak is Mauna Ke'a ("the white mountain") on the Big Island. It rises over 30,000 feet from its base in the deep ocean, several hundred feet higher than Mt. Everest. You can ski on Mauna Ke'a in the morning, and in less than 90 minutes be on the beach in the hot sun. Mauna Loa ("the long mountain") is the largest mountain-mass in the world (100 times greater than Mt. Fuji). Haleakalā ("house of the sun") on the island of Maui has a 21-mile-wide crater. A new island named Lō'ihi is being formed beneath the ocean just south of the Big Island. Scientists say Lō'ihi will emerge in ten thousand years.

V is also our Volcanoes National Park, a 218,000-acre preserve established in 1916. There are two volcanoes in the park, Kīlauea and Mauna Loa. Kīlauea has been erupting continuously since January 1983. Lava is the molten rock that comes from an erupting volcano vent. *Pāhoehoe* is a Hawaiian term for a lava flow that has a smooth surface, while *'a'ā* has a rough, jagged surface.

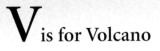

Vis for Volcano

Powerful shield volcanoes
made our island home.
Jagged *‘a‘ā* and smooth *pāhoehoe* lava
spew from cinder cones.

W

W is for Weather

The weather in Hawai'i
is always nice and warm.
The sun shines bright and winds blow cool
unless there is a storm.

People from all over the world come to Hawai'i in the winter to enjoy the beaches and tropical weather. The average daytime temperature in January is a warm 72°F and no matter what time of year, it never gets below 50°F. However, it does get really cold on the top of Mauna Ke'a, where snow caps its lava slopes. A warm wind called the "Trade Wind" blows constantly across the islands in an east-to-west direction. When four-masted sailing ships plied the waters, this wind brought trade to these isolated islands.

W is also for our words for weather. The Hawaiians had hundreds of words for each type of rain, wind, and rain/wind combination that blessed the islands. There were names for each cloud form or type of mist, and each kind of breeze. There was the chilling rain, the gentle rain, the slanted rain, the misty rain, and the rain that brought the rainbows. There were names for the wind that blew hard or soft or sheared along the mountains or beaches. How many different English names for rain and wind do you know?

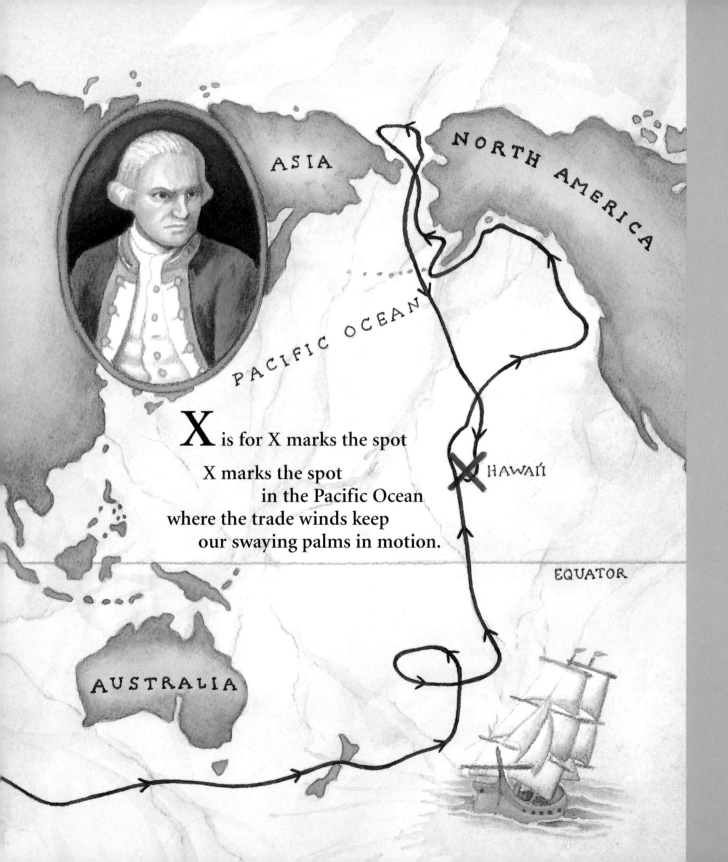

ASIA

NORTH AMERICA

PACIFIC OCEAN

X is for X marks the spot
X marks the spot
in the Pacific Ocean
where the trade winds keep
our swaying palms in motion.

HAWAI'I

EQUATOR

AUSTRALIA

Over 130 islands and atolls make up the Hawaiian Archipelago. Mark Twain described them as "the loveliest fleet of islands that lies anchored in any ocean." Stretching over 1,600 miles, the Aloha State is the most isolated population center on the face of the earth. It lies 2,390 miles west of the continental United States, 3,850 miles from Japan, 4,900 miles from China, and 5,280 miles from the Philippines. Hawai'i's land area is 6,422.6 square miles, making it the widest state in America.

X is also for eXploration. Scientists believe that Polynesian explorers landed at South Point on the island of Hawai'i around 500 A.D. Later, in 1778, while hunting for a waterway passage through North America, Captain James Cook stumbled across Hawai'i. He was the first recorded European to arrive here. He named the place the Sandwich Isles after the Earl of Sandwich, his patron. On his return from Alaska in 1779, Captain Cook was killed in a battle with Hawaiian warriors at Kealakekua Bay on the Big Island.

X
X

Yy

Y is for gods of Yesteryear

It took so many Hawaiian gods
to govern all of life.
They watched from temples made of stone
through day and darkest night.

The ancient Hawaiians worshipped gods and goddesses that ruled over nature. The four major gods were Kāne, Kū, Lono, and Kanaloa. Kāne was the god of sunlight, fresh water, and natural life. Kū reigned over war and all male power. Lono was the god of peace, fertility, winds, rain, and sports, and Kanaloa was god of the ocean. Lesser gods and demigods were Pele (goddess of fire), Lā (the sun god), Poli'ahu (the goddess of snow), Laka (the goddess of the hula), and Maui (the trickster).

Y is also for the color yellow, the sacred color of the kings. This is the color given to the island of O'ahu, which has been the seat of government in Hawai'i since the reign of Kamehameha the Great. Yellow is the color of the sun that gives life to the land, and it is the color of the hot molten lava that created the islands.

Because Hawai'i lies in the middle of the North Pacific, and because it is so isolated, it has its very own time zone called Hawaiian Standard Time. Hawai'i lies far enough south that it doesn't need to recognize daylight savings time, either. Hawaiian Standard Time runs 2-3 hours behind Pacific Standard Time, 3-4 hours behind Mountain Standard Time, 4-5 hours behind Central Standard Time, and 5-6 hours behind Eastern Standard Time.

Z is also for "zoning," Hawaiian style. In the islands when you are late to a meeting or appointment, people say you are "zoning" in Hawaiian Time. The old Hawaiians lived a very relaxed lifestyle. They started work when the sun came up, and went to bed when the sun set down. Things were very simple. When the Westerners came, they couldn't understand why the Hawaiians weren't on time, and Hawaiians didn't understand why Westerners were so rushed. So, in order to allow for these differences, they created a joke about "Hawaiian Time." When you're late (a little), it's okay because you're on the (always slow) "Hawaiian Time."

Zz

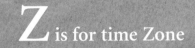

Z is for time Zone

Time Zone is our letter Z,
Hawaiian Standard Time, they say.
We see the final sunset
of every American day.

Q & A The Aloha Way!

1. What are the names of Hawai'i's eight major islands?

2. What are Hawai'i's four counties?

3. What does the Hawai'i State Capitol Building resemble?

4. Who was the last queen to govern the kingdom of Hawai'i?

5. What kind of fish is a *humuhu-munukunukuapua'a*?

6. What Hawaiian king was nicknamed the "Merrie Monarch"?

7. What is a *paniolo*?

8. What is the name of Hawai'i's tallest peak?

9. In the early 1900s, how did visitors travel to Hawai'i?

10. What are the two types of hula?

Answers

1. The islands of Hawai'i, Kaho'olawe, Kaua'i, Lāna'i, Maui, Moloka'i, Ni'ihau, and O'ahu

2. Hawai'i, Kaua'i, Maui, and the City and County of Honolulu

3. A volcano

4. Queen Lili'uokalani

5. A triggerfish

6. King David Kalākaua

7. A Hawaiian cowboy

8. Mauna Ke'a

9. By steamship

10. *Kahiko*—ancient; and *'auana*—modern

Pronounciation Key of Hawaiian Words and Their Meanings

'a'ā (ah-AH): jagged type of lava

'aha'aina (ah-hah-EYE-nah): old Hawaiian word for "dinner"

'Ainahau (eye-nah-HOW): Princess Ka'iulani's estate in Waikīkī

aloha kāua (ah-LOH-ah COW-ah): may there be friendship between us

aloha 'oe (ah-LOH-ha OH-ay): may you be loved

a'o (AH-oh): teaching

a'o hōkū (AH-oh HOH-koo): astronomy

'auana (ow-AH-nah): the modern style of hula

Haleakalā (hah-lay-ah-kah-LAH): "house of the sun," home of the sun god La

haupia (how-PEE-ah): Hawaiian coconut pudding

Hawai'i (ha-WAH-ee): "The Big Island"

Hawai'iloa (hah-wah-ee-LOH-ah): sister canoe to the *Hōkūle'a*

Hawai'i Pono'ī (hah-WAH-ee POH-noh-ee): Hawai'i State Song

hōkū (HOH-koo): star

Hōkūle'a (hoh-koo-LAY-ah): a replica of a Polynesian voyaging canoe and Honolulu's zenith star

honu (HOH-noo): Hawaiian green sea turtle

humuhumunukunukuapua'a (HOO-moo-HOO-moo-NOO-koo-NOO-koo-AH-poo-AH-ah): triggerfish

'īlio-holo-i-ka-uaua (ee-LEE-oh HOH-loh ee KAH oo-ah-OO-ah): "the dog that runs in the rough seas," monk seal

imu (EE-moo): underground oven

I'olani (ee-oh-LAH-nee): Hawai'i's royal palace

Iosepa (ee-oh-SEH-pah): newest voyaging canoe

kahiko (kah-HEE-koe): the ancient style of hula

Kaho'olawe (kah-hoh-oh-LAH-vay): small island off the western shore of Maui

Ka'iulani (kah-ee-oo-LAH-nee): Hawai'i's favorite princess

Kalākaua (kah-LAH-COW-ah): King David Kalākaua, the "Merrie Monarch"

kālua (kah-LOO-ah): roasted pork

Kamehameha (kah-MAY-hah-MAY-hah): the king who united all of the Hawaiian Islands under one reign

Kanaloa (kah-nah-LOH-ah): ancient Hawaiian god of the oceans

Kāne (KAH-nay): ancient Hawaiian god of sunlight, water, and natural life

Kapi'olani (kah-pee-oh-LAH-nee): King David Kalākaua's queen

Kaua'i (cow-AH-ee): "The Garden Isle"

Kealakekua (kay-AH-lah-kay-KOO-ah): place on the Big Island where Captain James Cook was killed

ki'i pōhaku (KEE-ee poh-HAH-koo): a petroglyph

Kīlauea (kee-lau-WAY-ah): Hawai'i's most active volcano

koa (KOH-ah): the Hawaiian word for "brave," and the name for the acacia tree

Kū (KOO): ancient Hawaiian god of war and men's activities

kukui (koo-KOO-ee): candlenut

ku'u aloha (KOO-oo ah-LOH-ha): my love

Lā (LAH): sun god

Laka (LAH-kah): ancient Hawaiian goddess of the hula

Lāna'i (lah-NAH-ee): "The Pineapple Island"

Lō'ihi (loh-EE-hee): new volcanic island forming underwater south of the Big Island

lomilomi (loh-mee-LOH-mee): to mash or crush

Lono (LOH-noh): ancient Hawaiian god of peace, wind, rain, and fertility

lū'au (loo-OW): common name for Hawaiian feast

malihini (mah-lee-HEE-nee): foreigner or newcomer

mana (MAH-nah): power or spirit power

Maui (MAU-ee): "The Valley Isle," trickster demigod of Hawai'i

Mauna Ke'a (MAU-nah KAY-ah): "white mountain," tallest peak in Hawai'i

Mauna Loa (MAU-nah LOH-ah): "long mountain," one of Hawai'i's active volcanoes

Moloka'i (Moh-loh-KAH-ee): "The Friendly Island"

Nēnē (NAY-nay): the endangered Hawaiian goose

Ni'ihau (NEE-ee-how): "The Secret Island"

O'ahu (oh-AH-hoo): "The Gathering Place"

pāhoehoe (pah-HOY-hoy): smooth type of lava

pahu (PAH-hoo): Hawaiian hula drum

pā'ina (PAH-ee-nah): old Hawaiian word meaning feast

paniolo (pah-nee-OH-loh): Hawaiian cowboy

Pele (PAY-lay): goddess of fire

pīkake (pee-KAH-kay): Chinese jasmine

Poli'ahu (poh-lee-AH-hoo): goddess of snow

pua aloalo (POO-ah AH-loh-AH-loh): the Hawaiian yellow hibiscus

Puako (poo-ah-KOH): petroglyph field on the Big Island of Hawai'i

pueo (poo-AY-oh): Hawaiian owl

pūniu (poo-NEE-oo): knee drum used to accompany the hula

Uʻilani Goldsberry

Uʻilani Goldsberry was born on the island of Maui, in the small town of Puʻunēnē (the hill of the goose). Later, her family moved to Lāʻie on the northeastern coast of Oʻahu. She has lived here ever since. Uʻilani has authored 10 books on various topics, including travelogues, cookbooks, and other nonfiction works, as well as three "Auntie Uʻi" children's books: *The Storm Dog of the Koʻolaus*, *The Shark Man of Hana*, and *The Night Marchers of Hāmākua*. *A is for Aloha* is her first book with Sleeping Bear Press.

Tammy Yee

Tammy Yee grew up in Honolulu, Hawaiʻi, where she explored tide pools, swam in streams, and wrote and illustrated spooky stories her teachers politely read. After she graduated from college she worked as a nurse. Having children rekindled her love for picture books, so in 1994 she exchanged her stethoscope for a paintbrush and she's been illustrating ever since. Tammy lives in Windward Oʻahu with her family, three birds, two upside-down jellyfish, and a guinea pig named Twinkie.